My First Summer Camp Before First Grade

The Adventures of NKKO

Nii Kunim Kabu Otubuah

Illustration By: Nii Tackie-Yarboi

WestBow Press books may be ordered through booksellers or by contacting:

WestBow Press
A Division of Thomas Nelson & Zondervan
1663 Liberty Drive
Bloomington, IN 47403
www.westbowpress.com
844-714-3454

Because of the dynamic nature of the Internet, any web addresses or links contained in this book may have changed since publication and may no longer be valid. The views expressed in this work are solely those of the author and do not necessarily reflect the views of the publisher, and the publisher hereby disclaims any responsibility for them.

Any people depicted in stock imagery provided by Getty Images are models, and such images are being used for illustrative purposes only.
Certain stock imagery © Getty Images.

Interior Image Credit: Nii Tackie-Yarboi

ISBN: 978-1-6642-8522-4 (sc)
ISBN: 978-1-6642-8523-1 (e)

Library of Congress Control Number: 2022922311

Print information available on the last page.

WestBow Press rev. date: 12/20/2022

WESTBOW
PRESS®
A DIVISION OF THOMAS NELSON
& ZONDERVAN

My First Summer Camp
Before First Grade

Acknowledgment

I love my mom and dad. I love my cousins.
I love my family and friends.

My mommy and daddy said it was
going to be a long summer.

My parents signed me up at the Young Men's Christian Association (YMCA) during the summer break.

We prayed together each day before
I went to summer camp.

Every weekday morning, my parents
drove me to summer camp.

I enjoyed the drive to summer camp.
Sometimes, we passed by the city hall, and
I liked to see all the big buildings.

And then my daddy signed me up for swimming lessons. It was a lot of fun to learn to swim.

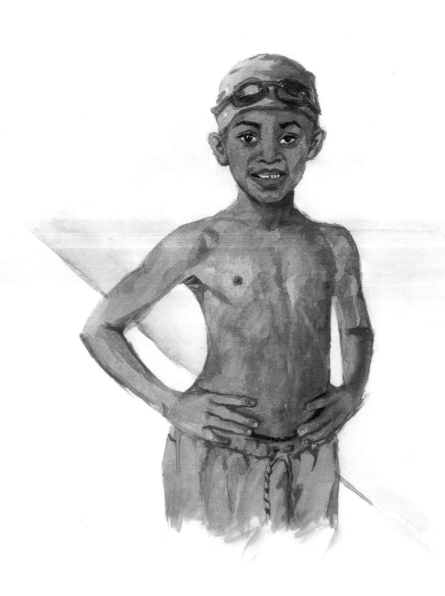

My teachers were amazing.

I learned different swimming styles.

I made new friends at the summer camp,
and we had a lot of fun together.

Soon, it was time to start first grade.

I was very happy to learn new things
and make new friends.

My first day at first grade was fun. I love to learn.

I love to play with my friends.

We had so much fun together.

Printed in the United States
by Baker & Taylor Publisher Services